Page Turners

Bigfoot

Julian Thomlinson

D1499215

Series Editor: Rob Waring
Story Editor: Julian Thomlinson
Series Development Editor: Sue Leather

HEINLE
CENGAGE Learning

Australia • Brazil • Japan • Korea • Mexico • Singapore • Spain • United Kingdom • United States

HEINLE
CENGAGE Learning™

Page Turners Reading Library

Bigfoot
Julian Thomlinson

Publisher: Andrew Robinson
Executive Editor: Sean Bermingham
Associate Development: Sarah Tan
Director of Global Marketing:
Ian Martin
Content Project Manager:
Tan Jin Hock
Senior Print Buyer:
Mary Beth Hennebury
Layout Design and Illustrations:
Redbean Design Pte Ltd
Cover Illustration: Eric Foenander

Photo Credits:
44 RichVintage/iStockphoto
45 Javarman/Shutterstock

Library of Congress Control Number: 2011909968
ISBN-13: 978-1-4240-4645-4
ISBN-10: 1-4240-4645-9

Heinle
20 Channel Center Street
Boston, Massachusetts 02210
USA

Cengage Learning is a leading provider of customized learning solutions with office locations around the globe, including Singapore, the United Kingdom, Australia, Mexico, Brazil, and Japan. Locate your local office at:
international.cengage.com/region

Cengage Learning products are represented in Canada by Nelson Education, Ltd.

Visit Heinle online at **elt.heinle.com**

Visit our corporate website at
www.cengage.com

Printed in the United States of America
1 2 3 4 5 6 7 – 15 14 13 12 11

Contents

Background Reading

People in the story

Sandra Marks
Sandra is a communications
student and editor of
The Brenton Sun
online newspaper.

Felipe Rosas
Felipe is also a communications
student and a reporter on
The Brenton Sun.

Symon Kotick
Symon studies computer science
and is also a reporter on
The Brenton Sun.

Big John
Big John is the owner of
Bigfoot House.

This story is set in the Cascade Mountains in the Northwest,
United States.

Chapter 1

Bigfoot House

It was a little after four o'clock on the first day of spring break when Felipe, Sandra, and Symon arrived at Bigfoot House. After five hours of driving, mostly on a small road up into the mountains, they all needed a rest.

The hotel was an old wooden building. It looked like it was about to fall down. There were no other cars around, and the forest was quiet around them.

Above the door, a sign said, "Welcome to Bigfoot House!" and there was a big picture of a hairy, gorilla-like animal next to it. Below, it said, "Looking for Bigfoot? You've come to the right place!"

"Tell me," Symon said. "What are we doing here again?"

"Looking for Bigfoot. Aren't we?" Felipe joked.

"I'm very happy to hear it," said a loud voice, as the door of the house opened, and a man came out. He was a tall and heavy man with long hair and a friendly smile. Felipe, Symon, and Sandra all said hello.

"I'm Big John. Let me help you with those," he said, taking the three heaviest bags into the hotel. Sandra went in after him.

"I think we already found Bigfoot," Symon said to Felipe, very quietly.

"Most people call him Bigfoot now," Big John said, "but the real name is 'Sasquatch.' It comes from the word *ses'qec*, an old word in the language of my people. It means 'Wild Man.'"

After checking into the hotel, Felipe, Sandra, and Symon all fell asleep. Now it was after dinner, and they sat around a fire listening to Big John. As he listened, Felipe looked around the walls. Bigfoot was everywhere, in photographs and news stories, though he saw they were all quite old. The photographs showed a hairy animal with two legs, a little larger than a man. Some people said it was bigger than that—up to ten feet tall. *You can't even tell it's real from these pictures,* Felipe thought. It was strange that everything was so old—as though time had stopped. Felipe wondered why.

"Why is this place so quiet?" Symon asked.

"Well," said Big John, "we close for the winter, and we only opened again last week. The summer is the busiest time. But not so many people come here now. It's hard to get here, as you saw. What brings you here, anyway? Are you really looking for Sasquatch? You said you were at college."

"We're all from Brenton College," Sandra said. "We're all reporters for *The Brenton Sun*, the college news website."

"Are you writing a story?"

"Well," Sandra said, "not really. It's our spring break now. I just want to see the mountains."

"It was my idea to come here," Felipe said. "I'm really interested in the Sasquatch stories. I read this was a good place to learn about them. These two don't believe them."

"I see," Big John said. He seemed to be thinking about something else.

"We haven't had reporters up here for a long time. The last time was for the Hughes family."

"Who are the Hughes family?" Sandra asked.

"The Hughes family . . ." Big John said, putting some more wood onto the fire. "It was about fifteen, twenty years ago. They came up from Oregon—Bill Hughes, his wife Mona, and their young boy. I remember them well—real nice people. That Bill Hughes, he'd been all over the mountains, looking for the Sasquatch. Anyway, they left their car here, took the trail up into the forests. And nobody ever saw them again."

"What?!" Sandra said.

"That's right. They never came out of the forest. People heard they were looking for Bigfoot, and the story got really big. We had a lot of reporters here after that."

"What? Did people think they found Bigfoot, and . . . ?"

"Something like that, I guess," Big John said.

"Did nobody ever find their bags or anything?" Felipe asked.

"Nobody found anything. There was a lot of rain—maybe that's why. You have to be careful out here when it rains."

"You know, maybe we could take their trail and see what we can find," Felipe said.

"I don't know," Sandra said. "I just want a break. Anyway, you know what I think about Bigfoot . . ."

"Sure, but we're going up there anyway. Big John, could you just show me on the map here?"

"That all right with you, Miss?" Big John asked Sandra.

"Fine," she said. "But don't expect me to look for Bigfoot. I'm here for a vacation."

"There'll be some rain Wednesday night or Thursday," Big John said.

"How do you know that?" Sandra asked.

"I can feel it," he replied.

None of them said anything for a moment. Felipe didn't believe Big John, but he didn't want to say that.

"So," he said. "Did you ever see the Sasquatch?"

"Not me, I'm sorry to say. But something's out there, all right. I'm sure of that."

Chapter 2

Signs

Over the next two days, Felipe, Sandra, and Symon followed the trail that the Hughes family took into the forest. They saw a lot of animals, but there were no signs of the Sasquatch. Now it was late afternoon, and the sky was getting darker. It looked as if it could rain, so they started to look for a place to put up their tent.

As they walked, Felipe thought about Bigfoot. There were lots of stories, and when there was a story Felipe always had to find the truth of it. Right then, he wanted to know more than anything: *Is Bigfoot real? You never know*, he thought, then stopped.

Below him were some tracks. Were they animal or man? It was hard to say, but they were big. "Come and see this," he said.

"What is it?" asked Symon.

"Can't you see?" Felipe said.

"See what?" Sandra asked.

"They're tracks. Look. They go over there."

The two of them looked.

"Are they tracks?" Sandra asked.

"You can't really tell," said Symon. "They could be anything."

Felipe took some pictures.

"You're just saying you don't see anything because you don't want to believe it," he said.

"And you're saying you see them because you *do* want to believe it," Symon replied.

"Let's just look for somewhere to put up the tent," Sandra said.

About half an hour later they were putting up the tent when a strange sound came out of the forest. It was the sound of something in trouble or pain, but it didn't sound like any animal Felipe knew.

"Hey, what was that?" Sandra said. "Was that a bear?"

"I don't think so," said Felipe.

For a moment, they just stood there, holding their breath and waiting for the sound to come again. There was very little wind, and the forest was quiet.

"It sounds like a bear," Symon said. His eyes were wide. "I thought they were all still in their winter sleep."

"Quiet, Symon," Felipe said.

After a moment or two, the sound came again. The only word for it was a moan—a long, slow moan. It didn't sound happy.

"Hey, listen to that," Felipe said. "That's no bear."

"It has to be," Sandra said.

"What if it is?" Symon said. He looked scared.

Could this be Bigfoot? Felipe asked himself. The thought was exciting.

"We'd better . . ."

A terrible cry came out of the forest, a long, howling cry that made Felipe feel very cold. He looked at the others. None of them moved.

"What *is* that?" Sandra asked.

Felipe didn't feel as excited anymore.

"Let's keep moving," he said.

They didn't hear it again that day. As they walked, Felipe thought about what Big John had said. A Sasquatch in Washington State sounded crazy, but a family going out one day in June and never coming back didn't exactly happen every day. *What happened to the Hughes family?* he wondered. Some people thought they disappeared because of Bigfoot. Could that be true? And just what was it that they heard in the forest?

These questions had to wait though, because right then it started to rain.

Chapter 3

A long, dark night

Well, Big John was right about one thing, Felipe thought. It was raining, and raining hard. So hard that it was difficult to see, even difficult to think.

The three of them were trying to put up the tent. It wasn't easy because everything was so wet. Symon fell more than once.

"This is . . . this is . . ." he said, but Felipe couldn't hear the rest because of the rain.

It took about 30 minutes to get the tent up. When they finished, it was already dark. They didn't want to get water inside the tent, so they took off their rain coats just inside the entrance. Even then, everything still got wet.

They were quite high up in the mountains and it was getting cold fast, so they sat close together in their sleeping bags. The rain hitting the tent was very loud. Symon and Sandra were shaking with cold.

"This is nice," said Sandra. Nobody laughed.

"Let's eat," Felipe said. "We can put the cooker on and use it to get warm. Symon, you've got it, right?"

"I think so," Symon said. He opened his bag, his hands shaking, and started to look through it. "No, one of you guys has it."

"I don't think so," Felipe said.

Felipe and Sandra checked through their bags.

"I haven't got it," Sandra said.

"You had it, Symon," Felipe said.

"I . . . I'm sorry," Symon began. "I'll go back and get it."

"Don't be stupid," Sandra said. "At least we've still got the food."

"I'm so sorry," Symon said.

They looked through the food to try and find something to eat. Most of it was dried—dried food was easy to carry—but without hot water, they couldn't really eat it. The only other food was a cold can of soup and some chocolate, so they ate those listening to the sound of the rain.

The rain went on for six or seven hours, then stopped as quickly as it had started. Now it was quiet, but everything was still wet inside the tent, and Felipe couldn't sleep.

"Are you two asleep?" Symon asked quietly.

"No, I'm not," Felipe said. Symon didn't laugh, and there was no answer from Sandra.

"Felipe," Symon began, "what do you think that was today?"

"The noise? I thought you said it was a bear," Felipe said.

"I'm thinking it didn't really sound like a bear," Symon replied.

"It didn't, did it?"

"But Bigfoot? Sasquatch?" Symon sat up. "Come on."

"I'm not saying I believe it," Felipe said. "But there are lots of things in the world we don't understand. Things we've never seen."

"Like six-foot tall hairy gorillas living a few hours from Seattle? That's crazy. Why aren't there better photographs? Why isn't there any video?"

"Think about it. You're the Sasquatch. Would you live near people, have them taking photographs all the time, making your life difficult? People aren't friends to animals, Symon. Hey, what was that?"

Felipe couldn't see anything, but he was sure he could hear something moving outside the tent.

"What was what?" Symon asked.

"There's something outside."

"I can't hear anything . . ."

Just as he said it, there was a loud CRACK. It sounded like something had broken some wood under its foot . . . something big.

"Did you hear that?" Felipe asked.

Symon didn't answer. Felipe couldn't see him, but he knew he was holding his breath.

Outside, the "thing" moved again. They could hear its slow, dry breath as it moved. It was coming closer, and the smell was terrible. Part of Felipe wanted to go and see what it was, but right then, he couldn't move. Sandra sat up next to him.

"What's going on?" she asked with a sleepy voice.

"Shhh," he said. "There's something outside."

It moved again. It felt like it was just outside, right next to the tent. Again, they heard it moan. That same low moaning sound they heard in the forest, but much, much closer.

"I'm getting out of here," Symon said, standing up. Felipe took his arm.

"Stay where you are!" Felipe said.

Then the creature howled, the same terrible howl they had heard that day. Felipe would never forget that sound—and he knew then that it *wasn't* a bear.

Symon screamed.

The creature howled again, and Felipe fell as something pushed against the tent.

"It's coming!" Felipe shouted.

But it wasn't. They heard it move, this time away from them. It seemed to run away into the trees. A few minutes later, they heard it moan again, but it seemed far away.

"Is it gone?" Symon asked.

Nobody replied. They were listening.

It was many hours until morning, but if Felipe slept, he didn't remember it. By the time the cold light of day came through the tent, he felt very tired.

At about five he decided to take a look outside. As he came out of the tent, he almost fell over something lying there. At first he couldn't see what they were, or at least he couldn't understand it. There, just outside the entrance to the tent, were three dead rabbits, all covered in blood.

Chapter 4

Three rabbits

Felipe looked at the dead rabbits and wondered what to do. He didn't want Sandra and Symon to see them. They would be scared, he knew. *He* was scared. He was standing there thinking about it when Symon came out.

"At least it's not raining," Symon said, then he saw the rabbits. His face went white.

"Sandra," Symon shouted.

Sandra came out of the tent.

"What is it?" she asked, then she saw.

"Oh, my . . . What are those?"

"They're rabbits," Symon replied.

"I can see they're rabbits!" she said. "Why did you put them there?"

"I didn't," Felipe replied.

"What do you mean, you didn't?" Sandra asked. "How did they get there then?"

"I don't know," Felipe said.

Now it was Sandra's turn to go white. Felipe thought he probably didn't look any different.

"You two are joking with me, right? Tell me you're joking," she said.

Felipe and Symon didn't reply. Felipe didn't know what to say.

"Someone put them there," Symon said. "That's why. Someone did it to scare us. Just like they made that noise in the forest yesterday."

Felipe wondered. He had also thought about that. But there was nobody else up in the mountains, or nobody they saw. It seemed that Symon was right about one thing though: the rabbits were there to scare them. But who did that? Or what?

"Maybe there are people who dress up as Bigfoot to scare everyone else," Symon said. "Like some kind of bad joke."

"What kind of people would do that?" Sandra asked.

"Crazy people!" Symon said. He looked like he was about to cry. Felipe didn't know what to say so he said nothing.

Looking at the rabbits made Felipe think about the Hughes family. There were three of them, too. *Did they get up one morning to find three dead rabbits outside their tent?* he asked himself. *Before they went missing?*

"Look," said Sandra. On the ground were more of the tracks Felipe had seen in the forest. They were all around the tent.

"Let's get out of here," Sandra said.

It wasn't so easy. They put away the tent and tried to head back, but the rain had made the trail very difficult. They soon found that they couldn't get home by going back on their trail. It was just too dangerous—the rain had pushed part of the trail down the mountain. Felipe looked at the map and thought about what to do. Symon was checking the GPS on his phone.

"Find anything?" Sandra asked him.

"It's not working," he replied.

Felipe noticed Symon's hand was shaking as he held his phone. Sandra's face was white. Felipe was scared, too, but he knew being scared was going to get them in trouble.

"I think we're here," Felipe said, showing Symon and Sandra on the map. "If we keep going this way, three or four miles, we'll come to the small river . . . here. We can follow that down to this road here." He showed them on the map.

"Three or four miles!" Sandra said.

"Into the forest!" Symon said. "No. No way. With that thing in there? Are you crazy?"

"We can't go back," Felipe told him. "If we go through the trees, we can find the river."

"I'm telling you," Symon said, "I'm not going into that forest."

"Can we do anything else?" Sandra said.

"Sure," Felipe said. "We can stay here."

"We're going," said Sandra.

They started walking and moved deeper into the forest. They moved slowly, partly because of the trees and the soft ground, and partly because they were so tired. Felipe kept checking his map to make sure they didn't go the wrong way. It was very quiet, and they spoke only a little, as if they didn't want to be heard.

Felipe had always liked forests, but this was different. Today he was scared, and he felt sure something, or someone, was following them. It was hard to say why. Sometimes there would be a sound behind them. One time he turned round and thought he saw something in the trees behind them. *Before Symon said I was seeing things because I wanted to see them*, he thought. *Now I'm seeing them because I* don't *want to see them.*

At least, that's what he hoped.

He didn't say anything to the others, but he could tell they felt it, too.

Soon it was midday, but there was still no sign of the river. Sandra and Symon were talking quietly, while Felipe looked at the map. *Where is this river?* he wondered.

"Felipe," Sandra began. "We think maybe we need to go back."

Felipe put the map down. He thought this might happen.

"Okay," he said. "Why?"

"Well, we haven't found the river yet. What if we have to stay here tonight?"

"We won't," Felipe said. "But if we do, then we have to stay here. Listen. This is the right way. I'm sure of it. We're just going slowly, that's all."

"We think we need to go back," Symon said again. Felipe tried to stop himself from getting angry.

"You know we can't go back," he said. "We could go a long way around, but it would take us days. This is much quicker."

It can't be much farther, he thought.

Sandra and Symon looked at each other.

"These crazy guys, they want to hurt us," Symon said. "You know that, right?"

"Symon, relax," said Sandra.

"They want to hurt us," he went on, starting to shout, ". . . like they hurt those Hughes people. Maybe they want to kill us!"

"Symon, quiet!" Felipe said. "You're not making any sense."

"I think we should go back," Symon said, quiet again.

"Listen," Felipe said again. "We can't go back now. I'm going this way. We'll find the river by two. If we don't, we can all go back."

"OK," Sandra said. "Symon?"

Symon didn't speak, but after a while he agreed.

"Let's go, then," Felipe replied.

Just before two o'clock they found the river. Felipe was so happy, he wanted to jump in it. They followed the river down the mountain. It was even slower going by the river at first, but soon there were fewer trees and it got easier. As they came out into the sun, everybody became happier. Even Symon started talking about what he'd eat for dinner when they got home. But when dinner time came, and the sky became dark, they still hadn't found the road, so they stopped and put up the tent for one more night.

Felipe wasn't worried. By now, he thought the animal was gone. They would probably spend this last night there, and nothing at all would happen.

Chapter 5

Deep in the forest

None of them were happy about spending another night in the forest, but there was nothing they could do about it. It was a warm, clear night, and even though it was still wet, Felipe and Sandra managed to find some dry wood and made a fire. While Symon and Sandra put up the tent, Felipe cooked some of the food they were carrying.

As they ate, they talked about the night before, and soon they were laughing.

"Your face when you saw the rabbits. It was so funny. 'What are those?'" Symon said, in Sandra's voice.

"You were scared, too!" Felipe said.

"I think we were all scared," Sandra said.

"Yeah," said Symon. He wasn't laughing now.

"You know," Felipe said, "I think maybe it was a bear. When you screamed, it got scared. It dropped the rabbits and ran away."

"Maybe," Sandra said. Felipe could see none of them believed it. *He* didn't believe it.

"But why three of them? Three of them and three of us, right?" Sandra went on. "Maybe Symon was right. Maybe somebody was trying to scare us."

"Who? You heard Big John," Felipe said. "Not many people come up here."

"Maybe it was Big John himself," Symon said. "Maybe he thought we'll write a story, get some more people coming to stay at his hotel."

"That's just stupid," Sandra said.

"What, more stupid than Bigfoot?" Symon shouted.

Felipe started to say something but stopped—he was sure he heard something in the trees.

"What is it, Felipe?" Sandra asked. There was no need to answer because just then there came a howl from the trees.

"Oh, no," Symon said.

"That's close," Felipe said.

The three of them looked out into the blackness, trying to see what was there.

"If it's a bear, we could sing," said Symon. "Then it will go away. People say that, right? If you sing to bears . . ."

"Stay close to the fire. I don't think they like fire," Felipe said.

"Can you see anything?" Symon asked. "I can't see anything."

"Shh . . . ," Sandra replied.

Felipe's eyes searched the darkness, looking for something moving. Was it here? He couldn't see it, but he felt it watching them. Waiting. Felipe wanted to run. At that moment, he was more scared than ever before.

Then he saw it: a dark shape, standing about five yards away, on the edge of the circle of light.

"Here," Felipe said quietly. "It's right over here."

It was large, about the size of a man, but Felipe could see it wasn't standing straight. It must be over six feet tall, he thought. *Is it a man?*

"It's a man. It must be," Symon said. "Go away, whoever you are. It's not funny!"

"Symon," Felipe said. "Please be quiet."

The creature didn't reply, or look like it understood. It just stood there, outside the light, waiting.

This could be a bad idea, Felipe thought, then moved toward it.

"Felipe, what are you doing?" Sandra asked.

"It's all right," Felipe said, more to the creature in front of him. The smell was *terrible*.

Maybe someone will jump out of the trees with a camera, Felipe thought. *We'll be on TV and everyone will laugh at us.* It was a nice thought, and Felipe found he wished it were true. *After all,* he thought, *better to be laughed at than dead.*

What do I do? Felipe thought. *Talk to it like a person, or like an animal?*

Getting closer, he started to see it better. It had long thick hair. Behind it, Felipe thought he could see its eyes. *The eyes look human,* Felipe thought to himself. *Or almost human.*

They look scared.

"It's okay," he said to the creature. "It's all right."

The creature moaned. Felipe stopped and turned to Sandra.

"Come over here," he said.

"I don't know," Sandra said, but she came over anyway.

"Oh, my . . ." she said.

They were both looking at it. It didn't look like a bear, Felipe thought. It didn't look like a gorilla, either. *If this is the Sasquatch,* Felipe thought, *I can see why they call it the "Wild Man."*

The body didn't look hairy at all. And was it wearing old clothes or something? He looked at the creature's feet. They were big, like the footprints they had found, and seemed to be covered in something. Was it plastic? And the smell: it made him feel ill.

"Sandra, can you see that?"

"I can smell it."

"Look at its body. What's it wearing?" he asked. "It's a person, isn't it?"

"Can you understand me?" Felipe asked. "My name is Felipe."

It came a little closer, but suddenly there was a white FLASH from behind them. Felipe turned to see Symon holding his camera in front of him. The creature howled angrily, and threw its arms up.

It's going to attack, Felipe thought.

"Down!" Felipe said. He pulled Sandra to the ground, face down.

Felipe didn't know what to do. He held his breath and closed his eyes, his hands covering his head. The creature came closer then howled once more and ran back into the trees.

For a moment none of them moved. Then slowly Felipe sat up.

"It's gone," Felipe said.

"I got it!" Symon said, smiling and getting to his feet. "I got a picture of it!"

Felipe turned to look at Symon. He was dancing about by the fire. Felipe walked over and pushed him, hard, in the chest. Symon went down.

"Hey!" Symon shouted.

"Stupid!" Felipe shouted at him.

The smile disappeared from Symon's face.

"But I got its picture. Didn't you want its picture?" he said.

"Felipe, leave him," Sandra said. "He's right though. That was stupid."

Felipe was angry.

"Don't you know what you did? Don't you understand how important that was? You made it run away before we could even get a good look at it!"

"I'm sorry," was all he said.

"Let's see it, then," Sandra said, sitting down next to him. "The photo."

"Okay," Symon said. He looked, then passed it to Sandra. Sandra shook her head.

"What's it like?" Felipe asked. Sandra gave him the camera.

In the picture was a dark shape. It didn't look like anything.

"Nothing," Sandra said. "We've got nothing."

Felipe sat down heavily.

"Maybe it'll come back," he said, but it didn't, and they never saw it again.

Chapter 6

Felipe's story

They left early in the morning and followed the river down the mountain. It was difficult, and none of them spoke very much. Felipe could see everyone was thinking about what they saw the night before.

But what was that, exactly?

He didn't know. He did know it wasn't a bear. In fact, he was pretty sure it was a man. *But what kind of man acts like that?* he asked himself. *What kind of man smells like that?*

Could it really be a man playing around, dressing up as Bigfoot and following them into the forest? He didn't think so, but it was possible. He thought about what Symon said about Big John: he's doing it to get people to stay at his hotel. Could that really be possible?

They came to the road at around twelve. They were all happy when they saw it and rested by the side of the road.

"I think we're about here," Felipe said, putting his finger on the map. "We can walk this way a few miles, and it'll take us back to Bigfoot House."

"Where we'll see Big John," Symon said.

"That's right," Felipe agreed. *And I have some questions for you, Big John*, Felipe thought.

In the end they didn't have to walk all the way. A man in a truck gave them a ride in the back. As the truck went down the mountain, Felipe thought about what to say to Big John.

They arrived at the house a little after one. Big John was there in the office, just the same as when they had arrived days before. He was happy to see them. Felipe was still thinking about what to say to him, when Big John said, "I hope you don't want to stay tonight, though. The place is full for the first time in years!"

And it was. A big group came from Seattle the day before. This all meant that Big John was in the Bigfoot House when Felipe, Sandra, and Symon were up in the forest. *Well, we know one thing*, Felipe thought. *The creature we saw wasn't Big John.*

Big John enjoyed their story, as did the Seattle group. Like the three of them, the people from Seattle were college students on spring break.

"Well, that's one of the best stories I've heard these last twenty years," Big John said. "May I see the picture?"

Symon showed him.

"Ah," was all he said.

Felipe could see the others laughing.

I'm not surprised, he thought. *We must look pretty stupid.*

The following evening, Felipe sat in front of his computer in *The Brenton Sun* office. He still wanted to write a story about what they saw, but he didn't know where to start. Sandra was asleep in her chair, and they hadn't talked much about it since they got back. He looked at the computer in front of him and thought about what he knew.

Felipe didn't think the creature was a bear, and it probably wasn't someone playing around either. Felipe thought about what Big John had told him. *"It means 'Wild Man,'"* he'd said. *That was exactly what it was like,* Felipe thought. *A wild man.*

"Did you write anything yet?" Sandra said.

Felipe jumped. He had thought she was asleep.

"Not a word. I don't know where to start," he said.

"I had a thought," Sandra said. "Do you want to hear it? It's pretty crazy though, I'm telling you."

"Go on. Sure I want to hear it."

Sandra sat up.

"I was thinking about the Hughes family. The ones that went missing. I was thinking what happened to them. Nobody ever found them, right?"

"Right . . ."

"Well, I read a little about them on the Internet before. Remember Big John said they had a son? He was four years old when they went missing. That got me thinking: what if something happened to Mr. and Mrs. Hughes? Maybe they had an accident or something. Maybe the mother and father had an accident, and the son was left all on his own. You know, you read these stories about children growing up in the wild? They forget how to speak, and live like an animal?"

"You're talking about feral children, right?" Felipe asked.

"That's it. Feral. Well, maybe the mother and father died, and the boy, Matt, went feral. Now he'd be, what, a little older than us?" Sandra said.

"Do you think that's who we saw the other night? The Hughes boy? What about his clothes?"

"His father's. It's a good story, don't you think?"

Felipe had to agree. It *was* a good story.

"What about the rabbits?" he asked her.

"Well, I thought about that, too," Sandra replied. "Maybe he knew we were hungry because of the rain, and left them as food for us or something."

"Well," Felipe said. "That is a good story, all right."

The problem was, Felipe knew, the stories about

children growing up in the wild were like the stories about Bigfoot: lots of people talked about them, but they probably weren't true. Felipe knew he couldn't write that. He knew he couldn't write anything without looking stupid. What could he write? Finding the truth of a story was the most important thing in the world to Felipe. What was the truth of this one?

You'll never know.

The thought came to him suddenly.

Was that true?

Maybe not never. Maybe one day he would go back to Bigfoot House and find the truth. But not today.

Maybe that's just how things are, Felipe thought: sometimes you can't know the answer, and you just have to tell the truth as best you can. In a strange way, the idea made him feel better. He turned back to his computer, and thinking about those wild, crazy eyes he'd seen in the firelight, Felipe began to write.

Review

A. Write the name of the character who said the words.

Sandra Marks

Felipe Rosas

Symon Kotick

Big John

1. "That's right. They never came out of the forest. People heard they were looking for Bigfoot, and the story got really big. We had a lot of reporters here after that."

   _____

2. "I'm not saying I believe it. But there are lots of things in the world we don't understand. Things we've never seen."

   _____

3. "I had a thought. Do you want to hear it? It's pretty crazy though, I'm telling you."

   _____

4. "Maybe it was Big John himself. Maybe he thought we'll write a story, get some more people coming to stay at his hotel."

   _____

B. Read each statement and circle whether it is true (T) or false (F).

1. It is Felipe's idea to visit Bigfoot House.   T / F
2. Big John claims to have seen Bigfoot before.   T / F
3. The students follow the tracks into the forest.   T / F
4. Symon forgets to bring food for their trip.   T / F
5. Felipe is the first one to discover the three dead rabbits.   T / F
6. The heavy rain made the trail too dangerous to follow.   T / F
7. They find their way out of the forest by following the river.   T / F
8. Symon's photo proves that Bigfoot is in fact a person.   T / F

C. Choose the best answer for each question.

1. *Sasquatch* is the real name for _____.

    a. Bigfoot

    b. the forest

    c. Big John's language

2. What does Symon mean when he tells Felipe "you're saying you see them because you do want to believe it."

    a. He thinks Felipe is affected by what Big John told him.

    b. He thinks Felipe is lying so he can tell people he's seen Bigfoot.

    c. He thinks Felipe looks for things to confirm what he already believes.

3. What scares the creature and causes it to run away?

    a. Felipe's attempts to talk to it

    b. the flash from Symon's camera

    c. Felipe and Sandra going closer to it

4. Which of the following is not a reason they realized Bigfoot might be human?

    a. It could understand what they said.

    b. Its eyes looked human.

    c. It seemed to be wearing clothes.

5. What does Sandra think happened to the Hughes boy?

    a. He dresses up as Bigfoot to trick people.

    b. He and his parents were killed by Bigfoot.

    c. He grew up in the forest as a "wild man."

Background Reading:

Spotlight on ... *The Sasquatch*

The Sasquatch, or "Bigfoot," is one of the most famous monster legends in North America. There have been many sightings over the years, and even some photos and videos. People say the Sasquatch looks like a giant ape and walks on two legs like a human. It is also very tall, between 1.8 to 2.5 meters (six to eight feet).

The most famous case was in October 1957, when Roger Patterson and Robert Grimlin filmed a Sasquatch in the forests near Bluff Creek in Northern California. They said that they followed it for a while, but lost it in the trees. The film they took wasn't very good and many people think the creature was really a person in an ape suit. But there are many others who believe it is real.

Most scientists say the Sasquatch doesn't exist. For one, they say there must be more than one Sasquatch around, or else it would never survive. And if there were a few, then surely there would be more sightings. Modern technology has also shown earlier photos and videos of Bigfoot to be hoaxes—something created to fool people.

But the stories continue. Maybe Bigfoot really does exist and he's good at hiding ... or maybe he just lives in our imaginations.

Think About It

1. Do you think there is a possibility that Bigfoot exists?

2. What other monster legends can you think of?

Background Reading:
Spotlight on ... *Feral children*

A feral child is one who has had little or no human contact from a very young age. In many cases, these children have either gotten lost in the forest, lost their parents, or were taken by wild animals. These animals take care of the child as if it was their own.

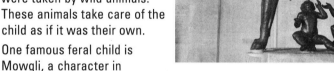

One famous feral child is Mowgli, a character in Rudyard Kipling's *The Jungle Book*. It's a story about a boy who grew up with animals in the jungle. Another famous story is of two brothers Romulus and Remus, who were raised by wolves and later founded the Italian city of Rome.

There are also many real-life examples of feral children. Sadly, because they have not lived with humans from a young age, many of them find it difficult to learn language or return to human society.

One of them is Oxana Malaya, an eight-year-old girl who was found in Ukraine in 1991. She had lived most of her life with dogs, so she growled, barked, and even ate raw meat. Today, Oxana stays in a special clinic and has learned to speak, but scientists believe she may never fit back into normal human life.

"When I feel lonely, I find myself doing anything. I crawl on all fours. This is how lonely I am. Because I have nobody, I spend my time with dogs. I go for walks and do anything I want to, and nobody notices that I crawl on all fours."

– Oxana Malaya

Think About It

1. How do you think feral children survive in the wild?

2. Do you think these children should be returned to human life, or left alone?

Glossary

bear	(*n.*)	A bear is a large hairy animal that lives in the forest.
breath	(*n.*)	Your breath is the air that comes out of your mouth.
creature	(*n.*)	A creature is an animal that is unknown.
feral	(*adj.*)	A feral person has become wild like an animal in behavior.
GPS	(*n.*)	GPS (Global Positioning System) is a technology to help find your location.
howl	(*v.*)	If an animal howls it makes a long, loud crying sound.
moan	(*v.*)	If you moan, you make a noise that shows you are unhappy or in pain.
reporter	(*n.*)	Reporters write news stories for newspapers, magazines, and TV.
scared	(*adj.*)	When you are scared, you are afraid or frightened.
scream	(*v.*)	When you scream, you shout loudly because you are afraid.
shake	(*v.*)	When you shake, your body moves out of control because you are very cold or scared.
sign	(*n.*)	A sign is a mark or shape that has a meaning.
tent	(*n.*)	A tent is something you can sleep in made of cloth and held up with ropes and poles.
tracks	(*n.*)	If an animal or person leaves tracks on the ground, you can tell that they walked there.
trail	(*n.*)	A trail is a path through a forest on which people can walk.
vacation	(*n.*)	A vacation is a period of time when you can relax and enjoy yourself away from home.
wood	(*n.*)	Wood comes from trees and is used to make things such as pencils and chairs.